One Thousand I Do's

One Thousand I Do's

by

Kristeen Polhamus

ISBN: 1-55517-506-6
v.2

Published by Bonneville Books

Distributed by:
925 North Main, Springville, UT 84663 • 801/489-4084

CFI Distribution • CFI Books • Council Press • Bonneville Books

Typeset by Virginia Reeder
Cover design by Adam Ford
Cover design © 2000 by Adam Ford

Printed in the United States of America

DEDICATION

A book for newlyweds, romantics and for those
who wish to revere,

remember and KEEP ALIVE their

marriage vows.

Also for my dear, very patient, loving husband.

"Love is dreaming happy dreams together...
Marriage is bringing them down to earth and
watching them come true."

"TRUE LOVE IS ALWAYS MUTUAL."

CHAPTER HEADINGS

FOREWORD

During the past ten years, I have been most fortunate to have witnessed some one thousand wedding ceremonies—as seen from the piano bench. I'm the pianist/organist who triumphantly played "Here Comes The Bride," as the entire room looked on with awe and wonder at this ultimate celebration of love.

I saw it all from my bench; handsome, patient grooms with eyes of adoration for their glowing, angelic brides. Happily, their marriage entourage was complete with excited bridesmaids, petulant flower girls, adorable ring bearers and nostalgic, proud parents.

As a privileged observer, I soon came to realize that the very choice words spoken at these ceremonies, so rich in counsel, wisdom and guidance, were so very inspirational they must be recorded and shared with others. Hence, I present the following copious notes of ceremonies strong in marital truths and recommendations for perfect bliss—beautifully featuring humorous rules, wise warnings, historical facts, sage advice and the very basic loving tenets of marriage.

These blessed ceremonies were truly fascinating, insightful and inspiring to me. May their unique, divine messages be the very same for you—in the pages of "I Do."

INTRODUCTION

"Dearly Beloved, we are gathered here today," as the preacher would say.

Welcome to the wonderful world of weddings! A glimmering, glittering white fantasy of divine fulfillment. And—the promises of love, the hope-filled dreams and the earnest aspirations to succeed in an almost impossible relationship of constant companions.

In my position as musician, it was enjoyable to observe the numerous, varied ceremonies for which I played. Fortunately, I was given the opportunity to witness ceremonies performed by judges, mayors, pastors, reverends, ministers, chaplains and countless LDS (Mormon) bishops.

Although each wedding party was alike in some respects, (such as the proverbial wedding cake and Uncle Bill, Aunt Sue and the grandparents) there existed a diversity with each bride and groom situation. Each had a unique life situation which brought them to the altar.

Here in Salt Lake City, Utah, I witnessed all types of marriages, from the very young to the middle-aged and the elderly. Also, there were cultural representatives from nearly every ethnic group and nationality.

My most memorable weddings have included military ceremonies, twin sisters (double ceremony) a handicapped couple, a re-marriage to one another, second marriages complete with children, country-western themes, and Valentine's Day (very romantic). And there was one Halloween wedding!

The average wedding ceremony appeared to be constituted by two individuals between the ages of twenty and twenty-five years. They were invariably young, joyful and as much in love as they knew of love to be. Each ceremony became a public pronouncement of a social, economic contract/pact with family and friends present to validate their love/faith pledge—legal, binding, love-filled union between one man and one woman, regardless of age, race or position in life.

CHAPTER ONE

FROM THIS DAY FORWARD

"Well, today's the day!" as the judge did say. "This is the man and this is the woman, two individuals now in the hand of providence. Today, both the bride and groom can be nervous together. Although I haven't lost a bride yet!"

"Who is your best friend? Well today I get to marry two best friends. All you have to say is: 'I do or I don't.' The words 'I do,' are the highest compliment you may pay one another. The choices you have made thus far will determine in part your success and happiness for tomorrow. Your courtship has brought you to this point, and now from this day forth you both receive a new life. Be thankful for one another! Smile! You are about to be united with the person you adore.

"At this moment you both epitomize beauty and love. On this day, you are born together forever more, a birth and an awakening. We shall rejoice in bringing two lives together, which shall eventually become one life. Marriage is a unifying of all levels. Neither is the man without the woman or the woman without the man. This is a happy and a solemn occasion. Happy because you are united together in a celebration. Solemn because this is the most sacred ordinance. It is a divine fulfillment from heaven. On this joyous day, it is truly an occasion to celebrate, for a bond will be formed here that will bring two souls together as one.

"True love brings people to this point, the marriage altar. For both of you, there will never be another day, month or year like this again. The ultimate date—your marriage day. Few things in life we truly remember, but we always remember our wedding day.

"To everything there is a season; a time to be born, a time to die and a time for your lives to begin together. Marriage is a heaven-sent directive. Through marriage, we attain our highest character development; for we learn and practice the traits of trust, understanding, sacrifice and total development. Marriage is a most honorable way of life.

"Marriage is the most wonderful relationship in the world. Angels are around and about us when we are married. There is no connection more sweet and tender; with more opportunity to grow. Your marriage is an infinitely potential relationship, which is only surpassed by your relationship with God. It is the most rewarding of all companionships.

"You are about to embark upon a wonderful journey together. Now your life changes, you are no longer alone. Together, you are going somewhere and this implies progress and shared values. As a bishop I cannot give you a guarantee you will enjoy a happy, successful marriage. However, you can give yourself a guarantee by remaining unselfish, committed and loving.

"Let it be said that no one can actually marry you; in the truest sense of the word you marry each other. I have no magic words, you and you only are going to make this happen.

"Everyone here has a prayer in their heart for you. Your marriage ceremony, today, is recognized by God and the constitution. Clearly, there are five words which solidly support your ceremony today: 'Marriage is ordained by God.' However, no official of the state or the church can transform you into a loving husband and wife, only your own commitment and affection can create the marriage bond. You must do and be what your inner voices urge you to attain. And, above all, love with all your being.

"Newlyweds are characterized by openness, optimism and mutual engrossment. With the act of marriage, love has made a circle and it is goodbye to the two children. Your main responsibility is to see that the other is happy, for you are both trying to create happiness always. He or she is perfect—perfect for you! Presently, you wish to be perfect for one another, you wish to become the ultimate in love and respect for the other. A wedding, or welding, is not just a social custom, but a union between two imperfect persons.

"A true marriage is based upon a union of mind and heart. Your marriage is breaking on the horizon like a rainbow, promising sunlight and safety.

"The most precious thing you will have in your life is being together. Cherish that though, because some days it will be a great challenge to believe just that! At this point, neither of you have any faults in the eyes of the other, though they might develop within the course of time.

LOVE, HONOR, CHERISH

"When you become married, you set sail on your own voyage together. Tell everyone else to get off the boat. No one should give you advice, unless you ask.

"Marriage is a spiritual oneness. Marriage is a center for emotions. Marriage is the most difficult thing you will ever succeed at. It requires a lot of effort—from the other person! Marriage is about the other person gently holding a little bit of your life and then kindly giving it back to you. Marriage is a merry age! Marriage is an unswerving commitment of two people to each others' continuing growth and wholeness. Obviously, there are two kinds of marriages, compatible and combustible.

"Marriage is an act of confidence. Marriage is love's infinite manifestation. It offers you the most intimate experience of your life. Marriage is what life is all about! Within your marriage are two people, two individuals, where the uniqueness of each is enhanced. With each passing day, honor the essence of him or her. For in this marriage, you will bring your own personality and spirit to continually merge with another. Consequently, it is all bound together with your everlasting love. Marriage is an internship you continually fulfill, it is additional schooling for a lifetime. Marriage is the most sacred relationship in the world and especially in the eyes of God. The marriage contract should be the strongest tie in the world. It is the foundation upon which civilization is built and the hope of the future. Your marriage is an infinitely potential relationship, which is surpassed only by your relationship with God. Marriage is a pronounced life sentence. Marriage is a worthy enterprise. Marriage is an honor and an art and a privilege. Marriage should be

6

entered into reverently, thoughtfully and with dedication to one another.

"Today, we are gathered to share in the joy of this occasion, but most of all to celebrate your love for one another. Today, you stand somewhat apart from all other human beings. You stand in the charmed circle of your love and this is as it should be. From this day forward, you should come closer together than ever before. Through kindness and understanding, seek the life you envision together.

"This is the first step on your bridge you will build together and build so well! Therefore, do not allow the suspensions on the bridge to snap.

CLEAVE AND CLING

"In marriage, there is a covenant of the heart. Honor and obey are the laws of matrimony.

"Covenants are promises, two-way promises. Your divine quest is to cleave, allowing no one in between—a joint interaction. The critical key word is cleave, meaning none or no other. To cleave is your first obligation. Cleave is defined as to adhere to firmly, unwaveringly to cling, and it is based upon loyalty. Cleave! Hold onto each other! Cling to one another for a long, enduring marriage. The bride and groom might say, 'We are cleaving!' A covenant is a promise to each other, irrevocably infinite.

AFFECTION AND UNDERSTANDING

"The biggest part of love is commitment, and it will all work out due to commitment.

"Love is not based upon circumstances but commitment. You are making a commitment to the realization of love. The vow of marriage is a pledge of everlasting, uniting love—whereby a bride and groom commit to share all life has to offer, the good and bad times, with unlimited patience and understanding. What a wonderful event when two persons commit. As you walk together, you will discover possibilities. The love you share together is the highest road to joy.

"Vows are remembered and heightened thereafter, when entered into with reverence and serious consideration. I charge you to enter into this marriage with both reverence and with laughter. You must have reverence because the love that you share is a gift from God. Only in reverence can you truly hold respect for the other, which alone yields to trust. Begin your new life with reverence and with a sense of awe for all that you receive. Also, begin your new married life with laughter, a life filled with joy; and let your joy bubble over into laughter, a laughter that stems from a sense of perspective.

"Commit, Commit, Commitment! When you come into this world, you are given a birth certificate; a piece of paper to honor and formalize your life. A marriage certificate is the same concept; one of honor, jubilation and legalization. A ceremony has nothing to do with love, a mere ceremony will not promise happiness. However, you may realize happiness by focusing on your vows with continual sacrifice and unending love. This ceremony marks the place you have come in each others' hearts. This day we express our emotions through the framework of a ceremony and then go beyond this ceremony with determination to fulfill these golden words.

"May I share a few important, valid thoughts for you to remember and lovingly activate in your lives? Neglect the whole world, other than one another, for your first priority is this marriage. Your basic success story shall be your commitment to each other. You share a vast future ahead of yourselves, so enjoy every moment! Use good judgement, make correct choices and have the highest intentions. Work at this relationship every day, to the remainder of your lives. The kind of love you brought here must sustain you the rest of your life. You have the rest of your lives to love each other. It is important that you love each other. If you possess pure love in your heart, it is not hard to love. Be happy to love each other. We each come from different backgrounds which is okay and perhaps even beneficial to your future children. It now becomes a high necessity to merge these traits and become a positive influence for one another. You both possess great qualities and abilities which complement each other, so use them advantageously. Don't try to make your marriage like everyone else, make it your own. Relax—and let your love grow!

"Cherish is a stronger word than love, because he or she becomes a beloved treasure to you. During the next two months, you will learn much about one another and also see the worst side of one another. So, if aggravated or irritated, get down on your knees and pray that his or her heart is softened, plus yours. Will you please listen to her? Try to live the teachings of Christ, which are tolerance, understanding and forgiveness. Live lives according to the Savior's plan.

"Look down both sides of these aisles and you will notice that everyone is present especially for you and this life-changing event. (Obviously, you must know by now that the family is your greatest resource.) Much thought and preparation has been invested in this day and the same should apply to your new marriage. This day is the beginning of a huge, great, colossal, jumbo, effort— coming from you and you. May all the persons witnessing this marriage today find their own marriage strengthened and revitalized with each passing day. A marriage cere- mony (a covenant with society) is a good review for the audience. Wedding vows remind us of the love in our lives. Your presence as an audience validates a social recognition to this marriage. To the assembled guests: Do you who are assembled choose to accept and nurture this bride and groom? To speak highly and avoid demeaning statements? To be loving and supportive? Friends and family, the greatest gift we can bequeath upon this couple, is to pray for them.

"I wish you a relationship filled with love and respect. Your merging as of this hour, proclaims an enfolding relationship. Your sublime attraction to each other, which has brought you here today, is the deepest mystery of life. Work at this divine relationship every day, to the remainder of your lives. Believe in each other to the utmost. Recognize God as the head of your home. Study his good word, for he is an ever-silent partner. This day, may you remember the words you say and the vows you promise to uphold. These holy bonds of matrimony declare your love for one another. In bringing lives together, you become one. A marriage is serving and being served, a marriage is loving and being loved.

"Victor Hugo stated, 'Life's greatest happiness is to be convinced you are loved.' Each day convince your partner of that. Hopefully, you will both love the other person for what they are, and not for what they appear to be. As you embark upon this journey, may you have an eye focused on happiness. Remember to tackle your challenges TOGETHER. May you share joy and sorrow and all that the years will bring. I bless you with abundant support from a loving God.

"Love is the reason for life and living. May your marriage withstand the test of trials and time.

"As you stand here before me, please hold up your right hand. The palm represents your marriage and the fingers are the family to be. One finger alone is weak, but together made into a fist it becomes united and powerful. Notice the fist perfectly fits into the palm of marriage.

"Marriage is a uniting of souls and a bonding of hearts."

Minister: "Do you choose daily to seek the truth? If so please say I DO. In marriage, be the complete, full man or woman you can be."

Bride and Groom: "I can't guarantee my strength, but I will always love you. I have chosen to give you the gift of my love. And I will share whatever I have that is good."

CHAPTER TWO

TO HAVE AND TO HOLD

(CUSTOMS, VOWS, HISTORICAL FACTS)

"The sacred relationship of marriage was established by God in creation. God is the author of marriage, bringing together Adam and Eve. The first marriage relationship occurred in the Garden of Eden between this premier couple. The mystical relationship between Christ (the bridegroom) and his church (the bride) becomes a significant comparison. Jesus gave up his life for his gospel and you two will in turn give up your life to be together. Our Lord Jesus Christ adorned marriage by his presence and first miracle at the wedding in Cana of Galilee.

"The apostle Paul chose marriage to symbolize the union between Christ and his church—and holy scripture commends marriage to be honored among all people. The union of husband and wife in heart, mind and body, is intended by God for their mutual joy, for the help and comfort given to one another in prosperity and adversity; and their nurture in the knowledge and love of the Lord. Let the husband 'revel' in the wife and let the wife 'revel' in the husband.

"Our Lord Jesus Christ taught us that at the beginning of creation, God in his goodness 'made them male and female. For this cause a man shall leave his father and mother and shall cleave to his wife; and the two shall become one flesh.' At the last supper, Jesus gave the commandment, 'That ye love one another,' which is the first law of marriage. When you sacrifice, you truly love. Jesus possessed this 'pure love,' for his sacrifice proved his true love.

"The word of God tells us what love is like and what love does. 'Love is patient, love is kind, and is not jealous; love does not brag and is not arrogant, does not act unbecomingly; it does not seek its own, is not provoked, does not take into account a wrong suffered, does not rejoice in unrighteousness, but rejoices with the truth; bears all things, believes all things, hopes all things, endures all things. Love never fails.' Corinthians 13:4-8

"A marriage ceremony becomes a sacred, holy experience. Besides being a religious ordinance, it is the beginning of a new family. Marriage is a commitment to God."

RINGS

"The origination of rings began with the Egyptians and the practice of symbolic ring giving. It was essentially a man's wealth reflected in gold. Gemstones began in the fifteenth century, when the Archduke bequeathed a marriage ring to his royal wife. Rings are an ancient symbol of roundness. Round, like an eye to see clearly.

Round, like the sun to shine warmth and love. Round, like two arms embracing. Look at your ring, there is no beginning or end, the circle expands and gives. The ring is a circle. If you cut it, it will have an end. Otherwise it remains endless. A ring is a circle of symbolism, representing family members and your unity with Christ. Your rings symbolize the nature of God. A ring is an outward, visible symbol of a continuing circle of never-ending love; their design tells us our love must never come to an end. Rings are a symbol of your married life, they necessitate a giver and a receiver. Rings are a ceaseless reminder of love's eternal qualities. Each time you look at your ring, realize it is forever round and eternal like your marriage. Though small in size, these rings are very large in significance. Made of precious metal, they remind us that love is not cheap nor common. Rings represent the purity of ore refined.

"What gift do you bring one another to symbolize your love? Rings are an outer expression of the heart. Your chosen ring signifies the strength of God. As you wear these rings, seek wisdom, tolerance, acceptance and joy. A ring is a sign of love and faithfulness. Your ring is a daily symbolic object of your love for one another—all over again. These rings should be a reminder of your special wedding day.

"As time goes by, the rings may become tarnished and somewhat dull. However, take it off and look at the inside of the ring and it will appear bright and shiny. No matter what happens to the outside, the inside of the ring remains true and vital. A ring is endless, new and sparkling, just like your marriage. As you place these rings on each others' fingers, you publicly deem this to be forever. May you who wear these rings abide in peace, love and togetherness. As you wear these rings, whether together or apart for a moment, may they be constant reminders of these glad promises you are making today. With this ring I give you my heart."

CANDLES

(THE LIGHTING OF THE UNITY CANDLE)

Pastor: "The two outside candles have been lighted to represent your lives to this moment. Both mothers light the unity candles and their action signifies the time they gave you birth. These candles are two distinct lights, each capable of going its separate way. To bring joy and radiance to your new home, there must be the merging of these two flames into one. From this time onward, may your thoughts be for each other, rather than for your individual selves. May your plans be mutual and your joys and sorrows shared.

"As you each take a candle and together light the center one, you will extinguish your own candles, thus having the center candle represent the union of your two lives into one flesh. As this center light cannot be divided, let not your lives be divided; but instead be the united testimony of a Christian home. The candles radiate light as Christ gives you light.

"As you each light a candle, that signifies independence. Now as you light a candle together, that signifies togetherness.

"Candles symbolize individual natures. When 'blowing out' candles, this represents becoming one body and soul."

ROSES

"Your first gifts presented to you as a couple, are these two red roses. These lovely roses represent your love for one another. Exchange these roses with one another, which becomes your first gift of love. Now unite these roses in a new home, this crystal vase.

"As a wedding gift, I bequeath to you a moderately-sized crystal vase. This is a vessel to hold the roses and represents strength. It is created to hold something, and is enriched by that which it holds. At this time you will be given a red rose. Go to the vase, exchange roses and then place them in this vase. During your married life, this vase should be appointed a significant place in your household. Each anniversary observed merits two red roses in this vase. At other times when one of you is experiencing problems and feels talk is appropriate, a red rose should appear in the vase to activate communication. So, therein, this vase represents wedding vows, mutual love and sweet communication. Please utilize this and grow to love this vase in the manner it was intended."

WEDDING CAKE HISTORY

"The ancient custom of wedding refreshments began in the 1700s. In Roman days the people would bake bread to be served at the wedding reception. The loaves of bread were baked and stacked into a pile. Later, during the festivities, they would 'break the bread' over the bride's head as a fertility rite. Another usage would be for the girls to take a piece of the bread home and place under their pillow to hope and dream about their future husband. Eventually, the English conquered the Romans and new customs were adopted bringing a sweet, civilized nature to the wedding event. Honey cakes were baked and later enjoyed by family and friends alike. Today, the bride and groom exchange (feed one another) cake and girls continue to sleep and dream upon a morsel of wedding cake."

COUNSEL FROM THE CLERGY

"Now your life changes, you are no longer on your own so hold fast to one another.

"Through God's light and love, your paths have crossed. The very best advice I can give to you, is to adhere to the principles of truth which are the embodiment of Jesus Christ. In essence, say and do the very things that Christ would always do. Build the solid foundation for your marriage by remembering the works and actions of Christ and incorporating them in your marriage. The precious love of God shall abide in your marriage, if you are faithful and persevering.

"Today we are gathered with friends and family to share in the joy of this occasion, but most of all to celebrate your love for one another. To have is to hold. 'Whenever two or more of you are gathered in my name—there is love.'

"If we love one another, God dwells in us. Love is the divine principle of the universe.

Pastor: "To this marriage bring the absolute best you have! I bless you to have a happy home, free of selfishness and full of devotion. Be faithful to one another. Look out for one another's interests. Happiness is a spiritual feeling born of truth and love, always found in secure marriages. The pride you now feel is a sense of belonging to one another. Marriage cultivates courage and strength, which in turn promotes spiritual oneness.

Reverend: "Now bone of my bone, flesh of my flesh—give yourselves to one another."

CHAPTER THREE

FOR BETTER OR WORSE

Timeless truths and choice counsel given to newlyweds:

"A loving marriage creates a 'perennial springtime' in your heart.

"What real happiness is becomes truly associated with married life. And, part of that is who you are and what you wish to become.

"Marriage is made in heaven, but maintenance is here on earth.

"Whatever effort you put into your marriage, you will become the benefactor. It is similar to a harvest, you cannot expect to reap if you don't plant.

"What you put into life is what you get out of it. (Quoted from Emerson). Ditto your marriage. Triple Ditto!

"Instead of giving 50% to your marriage relationship, give 199% and there will be no gaps, no gaping gaps!

"We must gain some proper perspective of the infinite and this is accomplished through marriage and day-to-day living.

"If you draw closer to God, you draw closer together. Marriage is a three-way partnership with God— a perfect triangle.

"Love is a constant choosing of the highest possible regard for one another.

"If you 'work' at your marriage, it will strengthen and keep you.

"Within a marriage, deepen your love and increase your faith and vice versa.

"Through marriage learn of faith and endurance; from becoming one in purpose and intent.

"In marriage, 'double your joy and half your sorrows' with this precious, new companion.

"Love is like yeast—it needs moisture and a warm body.

"In your marriage, remember to forgive, to overcome your weaknesses and assimilate your differences. Maximize each others' strengths—minimize each others' weaknesses.

"Marriage cultivates courage and strength, which in turn promotes a spiritual oneness.

"In an excellent marriage, you listen patiently and forgive freely.

"Consistently work towards an atmosphere of care, consideration and respect.

"Attempt to place as much time and energy into your marriage as you normally would into your career, schooling, sports interests and car. (Men, take heed!)

"Your marriage must have a strong foundation, constructed with good materials of cement, brick and steel. This takes time to build. Please do not allow a 'wrecking ball' (cruel words, vicious acts) to destroy this building of faith and love.

"Pull together instead of pushing apart.

"A life commitment refuses to be broken when things are tough.

"In a marriage be flexible as a rubberband. For from point A to point B, it will not be a straight line all of the time.

"Give and hear words of love each day. Giving and hearing these words makes all the difference. Listen to each others' thoughts, listening shows love and concern. Listen with love in your heart for your love is his or her inspiration. The happiest marriages talk through their problems. Speak words of encouragement and endearment daily.

"Make your pathway together one of light and love.

"Be kind, even if she treats you like a God and serves you burnt offerings.

"During your marriage days, occasionally 'take stock' of the positive things going for you and quietly rejoice in your fortune.

"Don't look for faults but for virtues. 'A soft answer turneth away wrath.' Quiet talk is the language of love.

"For a marriage to be successful, the other person's

needs must become more important than your own. Set aside your own individual selves.

"Marriage requires work, care and concern, which makes all things worthwhile in life.

"Couples with good relationships build a joyous, secure marriage.

"As a marriage partner, maintain a balance of compassion, humor and equality.

"A good marriage is: both of you not going crazy at the same time.

"Love that lasts forever is the greatest achievement any of us can ever have in our lives.

"Your service to one another makes a relationship strong.

"Give trust in order to have trust.

"Prayer sets you on the same path to love happily ever after.

"If you are a good spouse, you will do whatever it takes to make him or her happy and successful.

"For the best possible marriage, just marry a decent person.

"As the days turn to months and years, take the time to enjoy the little things in life—for each sunset or evening walk becomes a precious moment of together-ness.

"Do the simple and beautiful things that will make this love a treasure.

"Be unmoved in your devotion to one another.

Believe in each other to the utmost.

"An ultimate act of belief is believing in each other.

"Marriage lends a support to encourage willingness to face the tensions of life.

"Remember, each problem you share together makes you stronger, if you approach it correctly. In your married life there will be ups and downs and inside outs and backward flips and spin cycles. A marriage takes work—but the work is worth it.

"The 'big' things are the little things. Be polite, uplifting and encouraging, which are words of action.

"'I love you,' becomes hollow words, if they are not backed by truth and meaning.

"Keep your marriage alive—pay attention to each other!

"Do things on purpose, to bring happiness to the other individual.

"Do small things for one another, they are truly the best. Example: bring home fresh cut flowers, cherry licorice, diet coke or take-out pizza. Buy the milk when it has run out—be attentive and thoughtful. The small things delight, support and show you care. Find some little way.

"On your 'date night' each week, renew your dating covenants.

"Don't highlight in yellow the negative, instead underline in red the positive.

"The word criticism never built a partnership, painted a picture or improved a marriage.

"The biggest sin in a marriage is taking one another for granted.

"Be patient with yourself. This marriage business requires work—much work and practice.

"Always keep him or her on your mind by that kiss every morning.

"Tell him/her how special he/she is. Never doubt those magical words spoken.

"The marriage bond is not a burden, but a joy-filled responsibility.

"Be as pillars; stand apart—not too close, but spaced apart for strength.

"Married bliss is cyclic and usually not a normal, everyday thing. So become adjusted to ups and downs, ins and outs, plus great highs and lows in married life.

"Love is not meant for just two persons, but exists as a common energy to serve the world.

"Love gives strength to realize our own destiny. There is a power to you and your love.

"Marriage is a commitment of two people to each others' continuing growth and wholeness.

"Your marriage license provides validity, renders your union legal and gives support and strength to a growing relationship.

"Within this marriage, live your life with the courage to be a good marriage partner.

"Live in peace, goodwill and love, love, love.

"In a marriage, I suggest the groom become the

anchor and the bride will be the sail.

"We have a hope for loving and being loved. Love is magic, wrapped up with garlands and ribbons.

"Monogamy is agreed upon control. Marriage: a believing in one another to the end.

"When two persons love one another, they do not look at each other, but both look in the same direction.

"You begin your marriage as a painter does, with a blank, white sheet of paper. Will you paint an eternal masterpiece or a cheap sofa painting?

"Never go to bed mad. The contentions of today should never dawn on a fresh tomorrow.

"Never go to bed mad or stay up and fight! Do not let the sun go down while you are still angry.

"Your bedroom should not become a battleground. It is sacred ground. So go fight somewhere else!

"To be married twenty-five years without a fight or a cross word, shows no spirit. However, do not look for fights. They will find you.

"A man that can hold his temper has more time to hold his wife.

"We can't give to each other what we do not have. Each of you deserves the best from the other, so give and make it your best. We must give everything we are to someone else. Christ gave himself completely. The best gift to give one another is the gift of self.

"During the past few months you have said a lot of sweet things to one another–keep doing it!

"Never give the 'silent treatment,' instead talk to

him/her in a nice, calm, reflective manner and say the right thing! Remember these words, 'I'm sorry,' and use them often.

"If you don't talk about things (issues) you can't solve even the smallest problems. If you talk over the largest problems, you will have a chance to resolve them. Try listening to the words as they are spoken. Communication is knowing what you are fighting about!

"Communication, realistically speaking, is the ability you have in talking to each other.

"There will be numerous times when you wish to 'give up.' Only the deepest commitment and desire for longevity and loyalty, will provide endurance.

"You must have a commitment to the marriage and not to the 'mood of the moment.'

"Build each other up, concentrate on the good things, then the courtship is kept alive.

"The bride wants to hear: 'I love you.'

"The groom wants to hear, 'You are the greatest.'

"How to handle a woman? Just love her!

"Help each other be successful! Not I or ME but US—the two of US!

"Be even tempered, give and take, establish a holding pattern. Tolerate ups and downs with a good attitude. Be gentle to one another. Tell him/her, 'You're right!' 'I love you.'

"Use soft words, only use your loud voice when the house is on fire. If you hear shouting run for the fire extinguisher.

"Use low tones! If you feel you must yell, step outside and yell to the trees.

"If you insist on yelling, you must be too far away to be heard. Move closer.

"When speaking with your spouse, please use your eyes and ears more than your mouth.

"When the disagreements occur, please discuss it all by holding hands.

"For the many times you say, 'I love you,' please state your beloved's name first.

"Do this first, become very best friends. Friendship is extremely important. It will carry you through the rough times.

"The 'M' word—money—handle it wisely! Good, judicious, financial planning pays off!

"Monetary coins represent God's provisions to us. He wishes us to be responsible for money and our financial matters. If you wish to strain your marriage, go ahead and get into debt. Be aware that bills go through the mail with twice the speed as checks!

"Financially pay yourself first. When couples were married in the 70s, they were advised to not spend more then $30.00 without consulting together. Now in the 00's try not to spend more then $100.00 without the others' consent.

"There happen to be twenty-six different definitions of the word love in the dictionary. Practice them all.

"You have no right to change one another. You both shall change, but in subtle, different ways. Successful marriage partners honor one another.

"Without strength, you cannot serve one another. Without gentleness, there will be harm. Without humility, there is selfishness.

"Keep holding hands! Keep dancing! Marriage is an art!

"There is a word called love and the real meaning of love is the verb 'sacrifice.'

"His or her love knows the wonderful you and any great pain you may be suffering. Depend upon this and the support.

"Trying the silent treatment as a negotiation tool doesn't work. If differences occur, agree to discuss and then agree.

"How many of us are perfect? None of us, so therefore think before you talk and HOLD your tongue when necessary. I exhort you to become humble, caring and kind.

"Bride and groom, plant yourselves in deep soil and grow and bloom together, with deep roots.

"Love keeps no score of wrongs. There is no limit to faith, hope and love, three words which last forever, and love is the greatest of all. Love is patient and kind, never boastful, conceited or rude. Love delights in truth. Love gives not but itself and it takes not but itself. Love is resolve and choice.

"Sleep with a prayer of your beloved in your heart.

"The word marriage determines the destiny of nations.

"You are the missing piece of each others' puzzle.

"Definition of cherish: the little everyday ways of bringing joy to the other person. Showing your love by fixing, bringing, spending, talking and giving of your TIME.

"Love is not so much an emotion as an attitude.

"Love is the gateway to all answers.

"If there is husband and wife prayer, there is not much chance you will drift apart.

"Marriage is the greatest sharing experience you will have.

"It's all about being married and staying married.

"Mr. Right, you are the big moment in her life. Remember, an ideal wife is any woman who has an ideal husband.

"To misquote a former president: "Ask not what your wife can do for you, but what you can do for your wife."

"Make your wedded life come alive with trust, support, and love.

"You need to have the capacity to forgive and forget and then forgetting what you forgive.

"The true measure of love is how you treat each other during the hard times.

"Determine your wealth in not what you possess but rather in what money cannot buy.

"The greatest words in the Bible are faith, hope and love. Love being the greatest, especially in your marriage.

"May you always be pulling in double harness.

"No husband has ever been shot while doing the dishes."

"Whenever you are wrong, admit it. Whenever you are right, keep it to yourself.

"As a couple, you shall become one another's army and red cross." (Quoted from Dr. Laura.)

"Don't give up or give in. Give of yourself!

"Without love, we are as birds with broken wings, unable to fly.

"Look past little things and focus on beautiful things.

"This is a coupleship. There are two winners or there are none. Grow, learn and change while facing the challenges of life. Two can be a great team!

"To the Groom: Your number one job is to see that she remains smiling and laughing.

"Give 100% of yourself to each other and then you will be happy.

"Life is eternal and love is immortal."

CHAPTER FOUR

LOVE AND CHERISH

Rules, admonitions, facts, suggestions and romantic stories—for marital bliss.

"FIVE KEY WORDS TO INSURE A GREAT MARRIAGE:"

> 1. Selflessness.
>
> 2. Trust.
>
> 3. Forgiveness.
>
> 4. Communication.
>
> 5. Gratefulness.

"THE *LEARNS*"

1. Keep your problems at home and LEARN to listen to one another.

2. It is important to LEARN to know how to say "I'm sorry."

3. LEARN to forgive one another, quickly and completely.

Be number "one."

Become "one" in family.

Become "one" in ideas.

Become "one" in purpose.

THE *NEVERS*

1. Never turn to a third party, (family, friends) to solve your problems.

2. Never say you are sorry and not back it up.

3. Never resort to the silent treatment.

4. Never forget to observe special days.

5. Never forget to pray.

6. Never forget to use three words often.

"INGREDIENTS FOR A HAPPY, SUCCESSFUL MARRIAGE"

Two minds—for intellectual capacity.

Two bodies—for love and sensitivity.

Two souls—for trust, friendship and togetherness.

Two arms—to hold one another.

Two hands—to share the work.

One heart—that will love for all time and last forever.

"THREE IDEALS"

Loyalty—without this trait, you will not remain a couple.

Self-control—no other quality is as great! Practice this when you are angry.

Be courteous—your bride and others will greatly appreciate this.

"FOUR MARRIAGE THEOREMS"

1. Learn how to commit.

2. Share and spend time.

3. Don't try to re-make each other.

4. If problems exist, make a course change.

Bride to mother the day of the wedding:

"Now all of my problems have come to an end!" Mother: "Which end?"

"A LOVING MARRIAGE INCLUDES:"

1. Mutual Respect.

2. A Soft Answer.

3. Honesty.

4. Prayer.

"FOR A *FINE* MARRIAGE"

Respect.

Understanding.

Listen and Hear.

"TEN COMMANDMENTS FOR A SUCCESSFUL MARRIAGE"

1. COMMUNICATION—keep the door open and unlatched. Give 100% to one another, not 95%.

2. Do not take each other for granted.

3. Take time for togetherness "just the two of us."

4. Don't allow money to come between ourselves.

5. Respect—Consideration—Appreciation.

6. Have trust for one another, be true.

7. Develop and use your humor, one of the angels' greatest weapons.

8. Focus and remember the reasons you came "to be." Honor your vows.

9. Compromise must be part of your marriage.

10. Always, always be friends and lovers the rest of your life.

"MILLIONAIRE MANSION"

Pastor: "I liken your marriage unto a well-built home. Your love for each other is the foundation. Your loving verbal expressions are the walls of the home. Your actions and service you render to one another are the finishing touches of the home. What a mansion!"

"FOUR CORNERSTONES OF A MARRIAGE"

1. A sincere love for one another.

2. Trust in each other.

3. True devotion for one another.

4. There must be fidelity for all of these to go together.

"STAY IN LOVE BY:"

1. Your friendship.

2. Your personality.

3. Your kindness, a big heart.

4. Your gentleness.

"GREAT ADVICE FOR A SMOOTH-GOING MARRIAGE"

1. Have fun!

2. Learn to laugh at your mistakes.

3. Allow humor to be a big part of your marriage.

"Marriage is a 'three-ring circus.' Engagement ring, wedding ring and suffering."

"PERKS"

A woman judge giving advice during a ceremony once stated, "One of the wonderful 'perks' of your marriage is someone to come home to in the evening who will listen to you and about your day—someone truly interested in your supreme welfare and joy level. In actuality, one who views your needs equal to their own."

"THE EACH-DAY PHILOSOPHY"

1. Each day I will hope we shall respond to one another and give freely of ourselves.

2. Each day we shall not attempt to solve all of our problems.

3. Each day let us learn something new about one another and life.

"Adam was created before Eve, because God did not wish any advice on how to do it."

"Brides remember: The only child who won't grow up and move away is the groom.

"FINANCIAL COUNSEL:"

"It seems Benjamin Franklin, as a young boy, was sent to the store to buy provisions, but instead he was influenced by a salesman to buy a whistle. In late arriving home, he began to realize his great folly. His irate mother remonstrated him by disciplining him with the thought, "Don't spend too much on the whistle!" In your own marriage, be wise in your investments in cars, homes, etc.—"Don't spend too much on the whistle!"

"COMMON, PRACTICAL ADVICE:"

1. Treat each other as you would like to be treated.

2. Let your spouse "shine"—support and praise him or her. (Put up instead of put down.)

3. Offer positive, constructive advice in loving ways.

4. Neglect the whole world rather than one another.

"MARATHON STORY"

An athlete once remarked that he intended to enter a marathon and place high. He trained well, for he had much competition. The big day arrived and while competing, he suddenly became aware of a rock in his shoe. As he felt the pain increase, he slowed down but refused to stop. He was subsequently unable to fulfill his great desire. Failing to admit his problem, his terrible, injurious pride stood in the way and therefore he suffered a great loss.

Another angle to this story is: Have a plan, a flexible plan. You will notice this concept will become very necessary in your married life; for problems will happen, requiring action.

Also, there will be rocks—rocky times will occur along the way of married life. So, stop and get those rocks out! Otherwise if left unattended, the rocks will cause more pain and real problems.

"A SUCCESSFUL TEAM"

Fans ask: "Why are they successful as a team?"

A coach may answer: "It was my doing."

or "Independently, each guy was trying."

However, the real answer would be: "Together as a team we did it!"

"Success was achieved by blending efforts, talents and interests. Just as you will in your own marriage.

"OLYMPIC MARRIAGE"

"In later years, compare your marriage to Olympic participants and their characteristics.

"These athletes worked hard in their lives to develop: Courage, Persistence, Perseverance, Commitment, Honesty, Integrity, Patience, Endurance and Desire. Just as you will."

"NINE SUGGESTIONS FOR A SPECIAL MARRIAGE"

1. Remember the importance of your marriage.

2. Pray always, separately and together.

3. Avoid ceaseless pin-pricking, don't dwell on faults.

4. Keep your courtship alive, discover how!

5. Listen to your spouse, make the time!

6. Live within your means, stay out of debt!

7. Resolve your issues, compromise and always reconcile.

8. Share equally, home and family responsibilities.

9. Widen your circle of love with friends, family and interests.

PASTOR STORY

The pastor bequeaths the bride and groom with their first wedding gift. He then proceeds (using scissors) to cut a bill entirely in half. He goes on to explain this severed bill represents the concept that as a couple, they must make a joint decision to mutually use twenty dollars. For important major purposes, both parties must be in agreement to spend, otherwise twenty dollar bills will remain apart. "Tape this bill together—when you both concur."

"THIS SWEDISH PROVERB APPLIES TO MARRIAGE—"

"He who chops wood, warms himself twice." Translated: Make memories together, that you might eventually relive the happiness you have lived. Warm yourself again and again by remembering pleasant moments you have created.

"ASTRONAUT STORY"

An astronaut was headed toward the moon, when suddenly the control panel began flashing emergency lights of distress. The trained astronaut quickly realized he had been trained to handle and solve each problem, as soon as the distress lights began to blink. A parallel to this story is your marriage. When problems begin to happen (flashing lights), immediately begin the repair plan—just like the Jetson's.

"A FINE SUGGESTION:"

During each week, a husband should spend $5.00 on bread and $5.00 on flowers. Both equally important to your marriage survival.

"TWO FOR THE ROAD"

Marriage is successful only when a man and a woman stay on the same road and walk along it, hand in hand. God expects you to be on the same road, traveling the same direction.

"HEALTH PREVENTION"

These days, there exists a prevalent disease among us, known as the "I" disease.

The "I'm worried about me" disease, is infiltrating the world. Please avoid disease in your own marriage by placing yourself second in your relationship. Not "me" but "we."

CONTRACT VS. COVENANT

There are two kinds of marriages: contract and covenant marriages.

A contract marriage usually ends, because you "are not getting what you want."

A covenant marriage survives because there is no "I" disease and you are truly concerned about one another.

"These are all it takes: Love, Trust, Sincerity, Honesty."

"PRIORITY LIST"

Pastor: "Each day, please do two things to strengthen your marriage."

1. Tell him or her, "I love you."

2. Give each other a kiss—or as many as you would like!

A young, married couple sought out a marriage counselor for advice. He instructed them to list in two columns their likes and dislikes about one another. The bride began writing out:

1. Annoys me while eating grapefruit.

2. Leaves wet towels on the floor.

The groom began to write and then stopped and exclaimed, "This is all insignificant and doesn't matter." The counselor then stated, "You are correct! What is important is the relationship you are building, and keeping each other happy."

"THE HEART WORD"

H—Hear and understand one another, please listen.

E—Even if you disagree.

A—Acknowledge the greatness in each other.

R—Remember to give loving attention.

T—Tell the truth.

Have "heart" in your relationship!

Fact: Buying a marriage license offers no guarantee of success. It is very similar to a hunting license; not everyone brings home a deer.

BICYCLE STORY

Marriage is like riding a bike. The bike, as in a marriage, needs to be moving and going, plus it especially needs to stay up. It cannot remain stationary but is always in motion. It also requires balance. Balance in a marriage comes from setting goals and then honoring them with fulfillment. Goals include balance in job/careers, children, priorities and time considerations.

Incidentally, the bike will tip over if debt problems develop and self-centeredness prevails.

Occasionally, there may be deep ruts which will knock you off of your bike. When this occurs, get up, evaluate the situation, LEARN from it and then move on, bicycling together.

Keep Pedaling!!!!!!!!!

WANTED: ALL STAR TEAM

Requirements: Must have confidence in your team, leader and in yourself. Your leader is Jesus Christ and following his example will bring success to your team (marriage) and to yourself.

LOVE REMINDERS

Suggestions: Leave endearing notes around the house for your beloved to find. These shall serve to remind him/her of your undying admiration. Place these love reminders on the car windshield and in the cookie jar. Also, try taping one to the TV remote control. Why not?

COUCH VS. BED

Late one evening, a distressed wife was arranging a blanket and pillow on the living room couch. Her husband questioned her about this and her response was, "I am angry with you! Since we have been advised to resolve our differences before sleep, this is where I choose to be."

Husband's response was: "Move over and let's be miserable together."

"COMMON GROUND"

Together, couples should develop their mutual interests to the extent they need no other persons, places or things, other than themselves, to be perfectly content.

50/50

Some people believe a marriage is comparable to a 50/50 business partnership. Wise couples married more then twenty years, have come to realize it is largely a 51/49 love partnership.

WALK A MILE IN THE MOCCASINS

Whenever it seems your spouse is appearing irrational, unapproachable and in need of love, place yourself in his/her position, to understand the whys and wherefores of the behavior. And do not fail to realize that your beloved is down the road a mile, and barefoot!

FOUR RULES

1. The wife always makes the rules.

2. The rules are subject to change.

3. No husband knows the rules.

4. The wife knows the rules and changes them often.

THREE FACTS

1. There will be hard times.

2. There will be growing times.

3. There will be plateau times.

HUMOROUS ADVICE

Try this: Each week, one of you decides to take the odd days, another the even days. When it falls upon your day, you be the one to apologize and say I'm sorry.

"STORY TIME"

The quintessential O'Henry story of ultimate sacrifice, (where the hair is cut to purchase a watch and the watch is sold to buy combs for beautiful hair) is one of the greatest love stories ever written. Your marriage requires and demands this same devotion and loving care.

"THE NEVER EVERS"

1. Never ever consider striking one another.

2. Never ever consider divorce.

3. Never ever remain angry for over an hour.

"THE EACH-DAY PHILOSOPHY"

1. Each day, I will hope we shall respond to one another and give freely of ourselves.

2. Each day, we shall not attempt to solve all of our problems.

3. Each day, let us learn something new about one another and life.

"LOVE WITH UNCONDITIONAL LOVE"

1. There are no exceptions—only and always love.

2. Do not judge what is right or wrong.

3. Your time belongs to each other.

"PAUL AND CAMI (BRIDE AND GROOM'S NAMES) SPELLED OUT WITH SIGNIFICANCE."

P—signifies patience.

A—apologize and often.

U—united in love.

L—love and charity.

C—signifies communication.

A—amiable and kind.

M—much romance.

I—invest time, with no withdrawal.

"THREE IDEAS FOR HAPPY COUPLES"

1. Never give up!

2. Most folks are as happy as they make up their minds to be.

3. Keep on dancing!

"WHEN PROBLEMS OCCUR"

1. Think it through.

2. Plan a good action strategy.

3. Have PATIENCE.

"NEIGHBORHOOD CHILDREN'S STORY"

There is a story of the clever man who was growing very weary of hearing the chatter and noise of the local children. He initiated a plan whereby he invited them to come and play and be as noisy as they would like and he would pay them one dollar. The happy children were only glad to oblige and returned the next day to hear the man state the same plan, but this time receive 50¢. They returned again, only to be told they would be paid a dime for their same services. The children became discouraged and retreated, because it was no longer much of an incentive or a fun thing. The clever man knew the noise would end without rewards. Well, your marriage needs to have those same elements of incentive and fun. Find ways to promote rewards and reasons for joy, within your marriage.

A SUCCESSFUL MARRIAGE

With a marriage, sooner or later come the challenges of day-to-day living. Example: sickness, finances, differences of opinions.

Why get married? Two reasons:

1. You can accomplish more together than you can individually.

2. God decreed marriage for our benefit.

(Make it Successful By:)

1. Arranging time for one another.

2. Treating each other with kindness—leaving harsh words and sarcasm on the doorstep.

Judge: "Why are you getting married Mr. Groom?"

Groom: "She is special, I like her smile."

Judge: "Why are you getting married Mrs. Bride?"

Bride: "He treats me well and makes me happy!"

Judge: "Actually, you are being married because you both share the same goals and he or she must bring joy into your life. That is why we are placed on this earth—to be happy."

"What is your greatest goal? Happiness! If you get a good wife, you will be happy.

"If you get a good husband you will be happy."

"A WEDDING WISH"

May you have laughter, but not so much that people will begin to doubt your sanity.

May you have wealth, but not so much you seek riches. May you have love, because there is never enough love.

"BLUEPRINT FOR HAPPINESS"

1. Treat each other like royalty.

2. Practice self-control in speech and actions.

3. Courtesy—employ this concept each day of your marriage.

"THE KING AND QUEEN RULE"

Pastor to Groom: "Plan to treat her like the queen she is, for it is the key to your success. And, she in turn shall treat you as the king you deserve to be. If you fail to follow these royalty rules, you become selfish, which is the opposite of giving. Play the king and queen game often! Who is your king? Who is your queen?"

Happily married people sing this song often: "I'll get by, as long as I have you.

Ultimate, true devotion—The devoted swan immediately follows her departed mate in death, due to a broken heart.

THE SMALL THINGS

Small things build a lasting relationship, by making and observing traditions. Example: Together, purchase a new ornament for the tree each year. Or, vacation the same place each summer. On your wedding anniversary, seek out that first restaurant where you tried to impress each other. Consistent memories!

PASTOR STORY

I have noticed that the bride and groom are naturally nervous this special day. So nervous, they seem to be unaware of what they are actually signing in regard to their marriage certificate. So, taking advantage of their confusion, I stacked up some papers for them to sign and they are probably unaware their last signature just gave me a new motor home. Thanks, you two!

"FOUR THINGS TO CONSIDER"

1. You are forming a new union, do not allow anything or anyone to come between the two of you.

2. Sacrifice, for the good of the union.

3. Actively serve each other and then together serve others around you.

4. Recognize God in your union and in your lives.

"THE C's OF MARRIAGE"

Constant Consideration.

Constant Courtship.

Constant Companionship.

Constant Compromise.

Constant Counsel.

Constant Confidence.

Through time and perceptiveness (developed by you), your thoughts shall become as one. Eventually, before she thinks it, you will already know. Lucky guy!

"HOW TO KEEP YOUR WIFE HAPPY—

15 LITTLE WORDS

"I Love You!"—"You Look Great!"—"Lets Eat Out!"—"Can I Help You?"—"It's My Fault."

WITH CREDIT TO ANN LANDERS

Bishop to Couple:

"I wish you to imagine yourselves standing on the highest top of a mountain. Now, your vision is clear and superb. Later, as the years pass by, your vision might become clouded and unclear. Maintain that mountain-clear vision with the three words of communication and unselfish love."

"RESERVOIRS OF STRENGTH"

The state of Utah maintains a unique system of waterways. This is due to the mountain ranges and rivers which evolve and lead to lakes and reservoirs.

Your marriage is similar to a reservoir, representing service and security, reserve and strength—a continuous source of backup and supply to be tapped and utilized. Later, your children will become reservoirs of service and contact for you to draw upon.

"SOME ESSENTIALS FOR A HAPPY MARRIAGE"

Live the gospel of Jesus Christ.

Love and appreciate each other.

Develop self-discipline.

Curb temper and tongue.

Look on the bright side of things.

Develop, maintain respect for one another.

Give a soft answer.

Speak quietly.

Don't be selfish.

Look after one another.

Develop talents, opportunities of companionship.

Recognize differences.

Pay tithing, stay out of debt.

Develop ability to communicate with each other.

President Hinckley LDS church

INNINGS OF LIFE

Your marriage may be compared to a baseball player and the game of baseball.

Baseball requires teamwork and knowing the importance of your strengths and weaknesses. If you enter into the game without believing this, you won't last an inning or season. Your game (marriage) shall last a life-time, if you play your position well.

FINANCIAL PLANNING

"Loans and debts bring worries and frets." It is easier to earn and collect money, than to spend wisely. It is good to learn of careful money management! And, especially discover and cherish the big thing money just can't buy. Financial fact: You earn money and collectively pool it, now collectively spend it!

PASTOR:

"Words I would say to you are:"

ACCEPTANCE in each other.

RESPECT for each other.

CONFIDENCE in each other.

JOY in each other.

STRENGTH in each other.

In the play "Our Town," the stage manager speaks about new beginnings and how they evolve. The same concept applies to your brand new marriage and how you must desire a sound, mutual beginning so that you may completely evolve. Also, from this famous play remember life is to be cherished and lived fully. Never take it or your marriage for granted.

"THINGS THAT MATTER"

1. Thoughtfulness.

2. Sincerity.

3. Friendship.

4. Kindness.

5. Gifts of each others' love.

THE CORD THAT BINDS

Consider a common rope or cord. Notice that it is twisted in a three-way design, woven evenly together. You may compare this three-way cord to your relationship to God the father and his son Jesus Christ and you. Inseparable strands woven together so tightly, the cord can never be broken. Strands strengthen marriages!

THE GOOD BOOK

The Bible is God's voice speaking to you. You as a couple must use it unfailingly, for it is an important resource for your marriage. It will provide valuable examples and counsel throughout every circumstance you encounter. Please allow it to become your major reference source.

Remember, everything we have and enjoy and are continually given, is from God.

"RECIPE FOR A SUCCESSFUL MARRIAGE"

1. Choose the right person. (Correct ingredients)

2. Measure and mix, knead and blend. (Reflect and prepare)

3. Stir and fold, then arrange in baking dish. (Service and helpful actions)

4. Bake one inch apart for companionship, and that all the flavors may blend and become delicious in taste! (Enjoyable life).

FISH STORY

Some salmon fish are born high in the mountains and then fight their way back up stream. Your unique marriage shall require this same eternal determination. Strength and courage translate into the forms of love, caring and forgiveness.

TRAIN RIDE

Your marriage may be likened to a long train ride. Here we are at the train station, your marriage ceremony! Each day on your journey, there is a long train track which stretches out with endless possibilities. Obviously, there is plenty of steam, with sudden jolts, detours and derailments. However, at times there are beautiful vistas to behold and to cherish. Traveling there is half the fun on this "once in a lifetime" journey you began together.

MARITAL REINFORCEMENT

The story goes that a happily married couple progressed through the years, remaining married to one another. However, the wife was extremely concerned about their love and happiness, because her husband did not ever state his love for her. She questioned him about this and his reply was: "I originally told you I loved you and until I tell you differently, hold onto that thought!" The message to this story is constant reassurance and reinforcement are vital to a living, growing marriage.

BOY SCOUT LAW

If the bride and groom were to follow and live the boy scout law, they would find themselves in a wonderful marriage. "A scout is trustworthy, loyal, helpful, friendly, courteous, kind, obedient, cheerful, thrifty, brave, clean and reverent." And so is a spouse!

Words to paste on the refrigerator:

HONOR, CHERISH, COVENANT

Rules for Marriage: Look for the good before the bad.

Things You Must Have:

1. Humor.

2. Enjoy each other.

A Supreme Truth: Sharing is Caring and Living is Giving.

"SUGGESTIONS FROM THE UNITED STATES AND CANADA—FOR A LIVING, LOVING MARRIAGE"

Canada: Seek and instigate little surprises for one another. (Be spontaneous and place a rose on a breakfast tray with pancakes, then carry it to the bedroom.)

California: Spend time together! Drop the dish-towel and dance!

Oregon: Start and complete projects together. Cultivate interests that are similar—besides kissing.

Arizona: Maintain your Friday night dinner date.

"FOUR PROPOSALS FOR SUCCESS IN MARRIAGE:"

1. Practice flexibility and endurance.

2. Date each other—after the marriage ceremony.

3. Show forgiveness and tolerance.

4. Give respect and appreciate differences.

Pastor to the Groom: "Your ability to make her happy, governs the house. As she feels this love, she will mirror this love and return it ten fold to you. And remember, this woman of yours is special and different from you. A different good! She has the ability to feel intensely about a situation and have an inner sense about a solution. She is perceptive and able to detect and understand more than you are capable of perceiving. Seek and heed her advice!"

Loving couples like to sing, "until the twelfth of never, I'll still be loving you."

A TEN-COW WIFE

Is a cherished wife, because the groom was willing to provide ten cows for "her hand in marriage." Not content to offer her father the usual, small number of cattle, the groom in so doing lifted his ordinary bride to the highest level of adoration—thereupon causing her to feel, act and become a ten-cow wife. From this island legend, may every bride feel she is worth this price and may every husband feel exactly the same way.

AESOP'S FABLE

Your new marriage will come to resemble an Aesop fable, for each day you will personify strengths, weaknesses and foibles to one another. The moral is, you will gain experience and become wise, due to the love and patience from your beloved.

CAMPFIRE STORY

To the new husband and wife: The love you share may be compared to a campfire. Have you ever made a campfire? You will need a campsite, a bundle of sticks and some matches. Presently (on your wedding day), your campfire is a bright, crackling sight, with warmth and light. Alas, what happens when the fire grows low and dim and, with time it begins to grow cold? If love begins to cool, how do we rekindle the flame? A caring couple will place a bundle of sticks to revive the fire and think what these sticks might represent.

Number one stick: Talk to each other and listen.

Number two stick: Do things together and be there to help each other out. Share the work load.

Number three stick: Cultivate the virtue of patience.

Number four stick: Bring the Lord Jesus Christ into your home, for a sense of peace and happiness.

CANOE RIDE

"I equate your new marriage to a sixty-mile canoe ride. On this adventure there will be spectacular scenery and invariably some bland spots. Then comes the time you will experience rough waters and a possible capsizing. Will you have adequate swimming skills or will you falter in the water helplessly? Hopefully as a couple, you will remain safe due to your life-jackets, symbolized through love. Also, if your values are centered as one, you will not hesitate to throw a life preserver to your spouse, which represents a large wedding ring of safety.

THE TAJ MAHAL

The most beautiful of all tributes to a wife from a husband, is this timeless, magnificent edifice, long admired as a treasure. Twenty-two years in the making, sparing no cost in elegance and design; it was the ultimate expression of adoration. It stands as a symbol of the power of love, which as proven became greater than death. Ultimately, infinite love transcends beyond this life—as all loving couples know and trust to be.

"HOW DO I LOVE THEE"

In the classic poem, "How do I love thee," by Elizabeth Barrett Browning, the poet asks the question how, not why or when or if. How, is an active love verb, which if utilized well, will literally preserve your marriage throughout the decades.

CHAPTER 5

"HAPPILY EVER AFTER"

Pastor: "We now have the formation of a new family, please make God a part of it all. Your new home becomes a sacred haven and you must build a protective wall of values and unity.

"Unselfishness is the mortar and bricks are the unconditional love. Focus love to the other unceasingly and enjoy your new life! What we are in life is what we expect.

"A marriage that lasts continually develops the love and understanding that began this marriage. Marriage offers a solid source of strength to face life's trials. Marriage is the most wonderful relationship in the world, with the most opportunity to grow. They say in a marriage, a woman gives the best years of her life to a man. However, in a happy marriage, she gives those years to the man who made them the best.

"Initially, you both received a revelation from deep within, to marry this special person.

"In this wonderful marriage of yours, always follow that which is good and pray without ceasing, then live consistently with your prayer. Let your lives attest your sincerity. Through marriage, learn of faith and endurance, from becoming "one" in purpose and intent.

"Within this marriage, stay close to one another. Close enough to understand one another's needs. Marriage becomes a life-long service to one another, a tremendous challenge.

"You are what you stand for and your spouse will soon discover your "true colors" in this first year of marriage.

"Your destinies are now woven together. You now begin experiencing life together. Your life is filled with possibilities and your intentions should be a venture of faith and love. Your marriage will be a comfort to both of you. It provides a hearth, a source of warmth and light, from the outside world.

"The most important aspect of love, is the highest level of self-realization you inspire in one another.

"All possessions, relationships and earthly concerns require 'looking after or watching over.' Nothing neglected will thrive and this especially pertains to your marriage. Nurture it always and often!

"Marriage, is the most difficult thing you will succeed at. It is not about the ups and downs but getting through the day and later sharing that day with someone who cares."

"WHY GOD LIKES MARRIAGE"

1. It creates an appropriate atmosphere to rear children.

2. A husband and wife are able to develop their talents and skills.

"Say to each other often: May my heart be your shoulder and my arms be your home.

"Be kind to one another. That shows love. Smile at each other, that shows you are in harmony.

"Remember the vision you saw in one another and always believe in the ideal of each other.

"Watch for and anticipate the 'sweet seasons of renewal,' which occurs regularly in a marriage.

"To understand another's feelings requires curiosity, time and concern. Each day, you are both changing in a thousand subtle ways. Are you ready to endure and excuse what comes?

"May you always celebrate your marriage by your being together and sharing. Through sharing, the uniqueness of each partner is shared. Your combined love together will become a source of common energy.

"Make absolutely, positively certain you are first in each others' lives. Your special spouse comes first before work, children, deer hunting and shopping.

Bishop: "You have committed yourselves in love. Married life is a challenge and hard work.

"I suspect you will find this out. Have a love pure and single for one another.

"Marriage is a special relationship brought about as the result of a special love, and it can only be maintained through that love. Love is one of the highest experiences we can have, it adds depth and meaning to our lives. Love is a gift always to be thankful for.

"The wonder of marriage begins with a wedding where two people promise to love, come what may. The comfort of marriage continues with kindness and care that a couple gives one another each day. The blessings of marriage grow precious and deep as the dreams and desires of a lifetime unfold. Eventually, the husband and wife find the ultimate meaning of life in their beautiful promise 'to have and to hold.'

"The twists and turns of marriage will always be there. Try to allow room and time for growth in each other. 'Don't pull up a flower, let it grow.' Remember, husbands are like flowers, one day they will grow up!

"A good marriage, most definitely follows the 'Law of the Harvest.' 'As you sow, so shall you reap.' Treat each other graciously. Have a code of honor and follow it.

"In Webster's dictionary, the words 'friend' and 'love' are defined as 'affection bent upon admiration.' So consult your dictionary and commit these words to memory and usage.

"Your bride will become your best professor. Be open to her suggestions and ask her, "How am I doing?"

"Life is full of obstacles—facing them together—it is not as tough an obstacle course."

"During the ceremony, the following breathless words become apparent, 'You have chosen me.'"

"Out of all the hundreds of girls upon this earth, you married me."

"THE ALWAYS"

Always look for the good.... Always treat with respect.

Always be complementary.... Always know that little things count.

"Numerator and denominator, you are each a part of the equation. Be equal to one another's needs. Also, accept the goods and bads, the ups and downs and you will become resilient. This is a major quality you will need if you plan to become a parent!

"Do not wear a mould, fashioned by the other, that will cause pain. Be yourself. You are entitled to your own mistakes, which you had better learn from!

"Without forbearance, people tend to have short marriages. The 'thing to do' is marry someone who can stand you! Your spouse is a life-time friend and your partner for life. So, look for the good in each other and BE NICE TO EACH OTHER!!!!!!!!"

Bishop to the Groom: "Let her wash the dishes once in a while. When the newness of the marriage wears off, allow your growing love to root deeply through your kindnesses and discoveries of loving each other.

"You will discover that your marriage is your greatest source of happiness and your spouse is your greatest asset!

"It is easier to avoid problems before they can happen. Example/suggestion: Try to live with less than you make.

"There are three main events in your life: Birth—Marriage—Death. You have a voice in only one of these.

"A good marriage affords some of the most beautiful moments in life. Each day be committed to him/her and the real joy you share together.

"You are both 'number one' in each others' life. Please allow Christ to be 'number one' in both of your lives. Join together and allow God's power of spirit and holy unity to prevail.

"The truth is, love is the best feeling to have in this world. To trust your partner, to nourish the partnership, becomes the care and feeding of your beloved, which is of prime importance. The greatest gift is sharing love and laughter. Make each other laugh!

"Being in love is the very highest honor you can pay another person. And remember, when children come, don't forget you still love each other.

"Marriage should be approached reverently, thoughtfully and with dedication to one another.

Minds—Hearts—Souls

Today—Tomorrow—Always.

"Pray together, begin today and thank God you have one another.

"The Lord is the centerpiece of your marriage.

"Your marriage can and will wither on the vine, when there is no contact; emotionally, physically and socially. Love has to be fed in order for it to grow. Water is your care and basic communication are the nutrients which will keep it all alive!

"Flash forward fifty years and imagine—what do you expect to have in your life and marriage?

"All shall be possible if you follow the rules and avoid selfishness. Also, hopefully, you will plan to renew your marriage vows, fifty years from now.

"May your marriage bring you all the exquisite excitement a marriage should bring, and may this life grant you patience, tolerance and understanding. May you always need one another; not to fill your emptiness but to help you know your fullness. May you always entice but not compel one another, embrace but not encircle one another and may you often say, 'I love you!' And if you have quarrels that should push you apart, may both of you have the good sense to take the first step back.

"Marriage—a complete, unreserved giving of yourself.

"Your new marriage can be compared to a stream, calm and serene; not agitated or overflowing the banks, but smooth and placid, a beautiful mirror.

"Be certain to pray together and include Him in your decisions. There will be greater peace and harmony because of this.

"May you love through sunshine and storm. And—may the sun of many days shine on you two with warmth and light.

"KEY WORDS IN THE WEDDING CEREMONY"

Feelings.

Needs.

Understanding.

Wishes/Desires.

Working Together.

Humor.

Harmony.

Unfailing LOVE.

A LEGEND FOR ABIDING LOVE

Now you will feel no rain,

for each of you will be shelter to the other.

Now you will feel no cold

for each of you will be warmth to the other.

Now there is no loneliness for you;

Now you are two persons, but there is one life before you.

Go now to your dwelling place

to enter into the days of your togetherness.

May your days be good and long together.

Scripture: 1 Corinthians 7: 3-4

"Let the husband fulfill his duty to his wife, and

likewise also the wife to her husband.

"The wife does not have authority over her own body, but the husband does; and likewise the husband does not have authority over his own body, but the wife does.

Translation: "Baby, I'm all yours!"

Scripture: 1 Corinthians 13: 4-8

"Love is patient, love is kind, and is not jealous; love does not brag and is not arrogant, does not act unbecomingly; it does not seek its own, is not provoked, does not take into account a wrong suffered, does not rejoice in unrighteousness, but rejoices with the truth; bears all things, believes all things, hopes all things, endures all things. Love never fails."

Translation: This is what true love really is. It is not someone who walks around mad all day.

"It is someone who 'puts up with everything.' It is an unselfish, understanding, LOVING person."

Scripture: Leviticus 6:13

"The fire shall ever be burning upon the altar; it shall never go out."

Translation: "A fire should always be burning within a marriage. Thereby keeping the relationship constant and ever alive.

"Come on baby light my fire."

"CEREMONIAL VOWS:"

"I have seen the good in you, so I have more faith in humanity.

"Loving each other makes it possible to love others.

"Because you have loved me, you have given me faith in myself. Love brings life.

"I love through you and subsequently love the world. You make it possible to love more.

"The holy bonds of marriage are silken bonds, strong and gentle, unbreakable, yet yielding.

"'I love you.' The most powerful phrase spoken, is not good enough stated alone. You must show your love daily through your loving actions and deeds.

"Ground (base) your feelings and faith upon the Lord Jesus Christ, and you will have the abundant life. And—be unified in your efforts—for there are numerous opportunities for extreme happiness—if you are both on the same page! Go forth and abound in peace and joy.

"Dear newlyweds, ride off into the sunset on your white horses. You are his beautiful queen and he is your handsome knight in shining armor.

"And they lived happily ever after."

BRIDE AND GROOM

"I Now Declare You—Man and Wife!"

The long and winding road, or realistically speaking, a roller coaster ride of ups and downs, now lies before these newlyweds. All the excellent counsel and words of advice have now been spoken in these treasured moments of high anticipation and honorable intentions. However, if the wedding bells of truth be known, these two will basically operate from their natural instinct/temperaments and especially from their previous backgrounds and value systems.

From my musical perch of ten years, I have concluded the true operative words to live by in a content, fulfilled marriage are: Commitment, Communication, Consideration, Cooperation and Compromise. Please notice the word love is not listed because the word love is largely contained within all of the above.

The bottom line is: once the champagne bubbles have popped, the wedding cake has become stale and the bride has discovered the groom doesn't know the meaning of the word clothes hamper—real commitment to one another and to those vows will assist these "two" well on the road to their tenth anniversary.

The young "stars in their eyes" couple, have no concept of the years to come; bringing pain, disease, financial upset and dull Tuesday nights. That is when the C words will need to kick in with a capital, underlined C! Remembering and applying these words and these golden thoughts contained in this book, will produce a merger instead of a cancellation relationship.

"In later years, it is amazing to think of the arc of so much of a life spent together: the early exhilaration, the unfulfilled expectations, the inevitable adjustments and compromises, the recommitment to the relationship and comfortable settling in for the duration with someone you know so well" (Barbara Bannon). May this happen for all married couples.

In retrospect, it was highly enjoyable and gratifying to be a part of these choice weddings. My own marriage has been enriched and reinforced by these words of solid, heavenly counsel.

During these weddings (while playing the Wagner Processional and the Mendelssohn Recessional), my musical fingers always attempted to convey a "Best wishes for a joyous, successful married life!" Now through this special book—I wish it for everyone!!

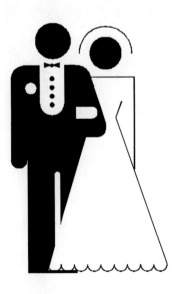

BIOGRAPHY

Kristeen Polhamus is a resident of Salt Lake City, and a native of Utah.

A past Sterling Scholar in music, she is a scholarship graduate of Weber State University, Bachelor of Science degree. She is a professional pianist, organist and violinist. A frequent performer in hotels, restaurants and wedding reception centers, she is a studio musician and a member of symphonies and a string quartet.

Kristeen is the author of "Preparing Perfect Pianists" (a guideline for teachers) and the writer of a children's book, "The Piano Lesson Cat." Her musical compositions are featured in book and tape (sacred) CD (contemporary) and piano solos (sheet music.) She is a published poet and has placed first in American Pen Women contests and Salt Lake Valley chapters of writers.

She excels in calligraphy, reading and teaching thirty piano students weekly.

In February of 1977, she married the love of her life, Gene. They are the parents of four children.

To all Brides and Grooms
Eternal Friends

Caroldine Gilbert

Kristeen Polhamus

searched   sad- ly think- ing you would   nev- er   pass   this   way.

So   man- y   years   suf- fered si- lent- ly,   look- ing   for   you   e- ter- nal

friend.   Then, hea- vens an- gels   joined   us   for- ev- er   our   search   did

end. The path we chose, is a des- ti- ny of light, for joy and

ha- pi- ness are now with- in our sight. We had tru- ly much to

face a- lone and fear, ad- ver- si- ty and op- po- si- tion

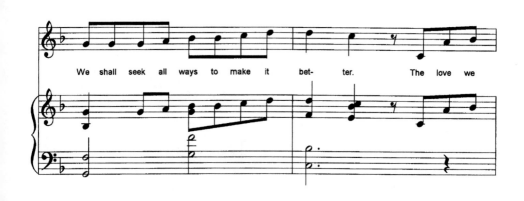

con- stant- ly were near.   This   test on earth is our's to-   geth-   er.

We shall seek all ways to make it bet-   ter.   The love we

share is a dream, an end- less plan.   Stri- ving as one, we can serve our fel- low

man. I trust and care, al- ways my e- ter- nal friend, you are the

one I shall love un- til the end.